STANDARDS FOR LIBRARY FUNCTIONS AT THE STATE LEVEL

by STANDARDS REVISION COMMITTEE
AMERICAN ASSOCIATION OF STATE LIBRARIES
AMERICAN LIBRARY ASSOCIATION

Revision of the 1963 Edition
Adopted by the membership
at the Annual Meeting,
June 22, 1969

D0503283

AMERICAN LIBRARY ASSOCIATION
Chicago 1970

Standard Book Number 8389-3009-3 (1970)
Library of Congress Catalog Card Number 79-99512
Copyright © 1970 by the American Library Association
Printed in the United States of America

CONTENTS

STANDARDS REVISION COMMITTEE
AMERICAN ASSOCIATION OF STATE LIBRARIES
AMERICAN LIBRARY ASSOCIATION

MISS ALICE M. CAHILL
Assistant Director, Bureau of Library Extension,
Massachusetts Department of Education

MISS VIVIAN B. CAZAYOUX
Library Consultant, Louisiana State Library

MISS DOROTHY R. CUTLER
Director, Library Development, Washington State Library

MR. ERNEST E. DOERSCHUK, JR.
State Librarian, Pennsylvania State Library

MRS. ELIZABETH H. HUGHEY
Chief, Library Program and Facilities Branch, Division
of Library Programs, United States Office of Education

MRS. JANET Z. McKINLAY
Head, Public and School Library Services Bureau,
Division of the State Library, Archives and History,
New Jersey State Department of Education

MISS ELIZABETH G. MYER, *Chairman*
Director, Rhode Island Department of
State Library Services

MR. JOHN A. HUMPHRY, *Ex-Officio: President, American*
  Association of State Libraries
Assistant Commissioner for Libraries, New York
State Education Department

MISS ELEANOR A. FERGUSON, *Resource Officer*
Executive Secretary, American Association of State Libraries

PREFACE

The first edition of STANDARDS FOR LIBRARY FUNCTIONS AT THE STATE LEVEL appeared in 1963, following six years of intensive study and research which included the 1960–62 national survey of state library agencies begun by Dr. Robert D. Leigh and completed by Dr. Phillip Monypenny under a Carnegie Corporation grant.

When the 1963 STANDARDS appeared, the president of the American Association of State Libraries appointed a standards evaluation committee "to make a continuous review of the 'Standards for Library Functions at the State Level' with an annual progress report beginning at the annual meeting in 1964, and with a report recommending needed changes in 1967." This committee, headed successively by Mrs. Elizabeth Hughey and Mr. Ernest E. Doerschuk, Jr., carried out the above assignment, and its final report became a starting point for the present Standards Revision Committee, which was activated by President Estellene P. Walker in January, 1968.

Intensive work sessions were held by the Standards Revision Committee in 1968 and early 1969. Its deliberations included suggestions and comments from many sources outside the committee itself, and the committee is grateful for this assistance. The present STANDARDS reflect certain changes in the state and national library scene since 1963. That the revisions are so few is a tribute to the soundness of the original document.

ELIZABETH G. MYER, *Chairman*

INTRODUCTION

Standards for library functions at the state level[1] are devised for the purpose of defining and clarifying roles, establishing goals, and presenting the guidelines for attainment. Primary in the statement of such standards should be a clear directive for the state library agency to assume a leadership role; for the agency to be in the forefront in planning, conceiving, initiating, directing, and inspiring.

The state library agency is impelled by both need and opportunity. The proliferation of material and simultaneously the possibility of the loss or extinction of records, the swift development of the automation and communication fields, and the continuous involvement with social, political, and economic forces with which it must be identified demand attention and appropriate action. The state library agency must be capable of developing personnel, programs, and the processes which will result in the highest quality of total statewide library service, which at the same time can accelerate a national information system. A prime responsibility is attaining sufficient funds to finance this adequate type of library service.

Implicit in this enumeration of *Standards for Library Functions at the State Level* is the charge to the state library agency of its responsibility for assuring that certain services and certain accomplishments are provided at the state level.

These standards are issued with the expectation that they will be used in conjunction with standards promulgated at various times for the various categories of library service. There needs to be a continuous sharing of information and a reviewing of library standards in all aspects of service, to bring about the greatest possible correlation, coordination, and mutual assistance in achieving goals of service. State

[1] The term *state* also refers to province, commonwealth, or territory.

library agencies must be conversant with and lead in the development and promotion of all library standards.

The state library agency must ensure that library functions essential to each state are performed. It maintains lines of rapid communication of information on the plans being developed at the national level by the American Library Association, the U.S. Office of Education, the Library of Congress, and other national libraries, as well as those being initiated and developed regionally and internationally. It assesses these developments and informs library interests within its own state of such matters. It works with its own library interests to utilize appropriate means of advancement projected by such outside-state interests, whenever they are relevant and applicable within-state.

The mandate to the Standards Revision Committee was simply to review and update *Standards for Library Functions at the State Level*. In the light of the National Advisory Commission's recommendations and the virtual revolution of library service (although the Advisory Commission itself says it should be evolutionary), it is conceivable that in a few years a truly iconoclastic, imaginative, and revolutionary document will be asked of the American Association of State Libraries. In the present state of the art, the committee felt that a fairly close adherence to the original mandate was requisite and right. The final recommendation of the National Advisory Commission on Libraries, "Strengthening State library agencies to overcome deficiencies in fulfilling their current functions," is significant. These standards reaffirm the spirit of this cogent recommendation.

CHAPTER I

THE STATE AND STATEWIDE LIBRARY DEVELOPMENT

The informational needs of today's citizen require a diversity of resources and services easily accessible. A strong library agency at the state level must have the legal authority and financial support to respond to the consumer's need through a coordinated statewide library system. This calls for an agency which leads, participates in, and coordinates the total library planning and development within the state.

Various types of libraries and agencies have been established by the states to carry out library functions. In this document, the term *state library agency* refers to the appropriate unit of government responsible for the function specified in each standard.

1. *The state library agency, in fulfilling its responsibilities at the state level, must ensure that library functions essential to each state are achieved.*

    The state library agency should adopt and carry out a role of leadership that permits maintenance of an overall view of library functions within the state. From its responsible, administrative preeminence, it should make certain that the full range of library services necessary to a state are assumed by appropriate agencies possessing the capability, local or state, individually or in combination.

2. *The state library agency should exercise leadership and participate in the development of statewide plans involving all types of libraries at all levels within the state. It should take the initiative in marshalling*

*qualified individuals, groups, and agencies to engage in such overall
planning.*

Planning means a concept of comprehensive library service, the
levels of facilities to meet the needs of the state, and the money to
provide these facilities. It presupposes the development of a climate
of assent and consent among the participants. Planning should be done
in conjunction with the statewide library development groups. The
state library agency should stimulate as well as coordinate the planning
and assist in it. All library and related education leaders should be
encouraged to question, suggest, and react to any proposed plan. In
every state it should be possible to document the present and coming
needs for library service; the kinds of services, information, and resources necessary to meet these needs; and the character of coordinated
library services for every citizen.

3. *The state library agency should review continuously both federal and
state legislation affecting library service in order to ensure compatibility
and to maintain a legal climate conducive to total library growth and
development.*

Most library service derives from state law supplemented by federal
law. In addition, there are the general laws—for personnel, for financial
operation—which affect libraries as well as other government offices.
In particular, state legislation should permit the types of library structure—countywide, regional, federated, cooperative, and contractual
agreements—called for in the state development plan (see Standard 2).
If the library laws within the state are archaic and restrict library development, it is the state library agency which carries major responsibility for modernization.

The role of the state agency should be strengthened by strong legal
and financial provisions which recognize the educational function of
statewide library service.

4. *The state library agency should encourage and facilitate cooperative
library services across state lines through interstate library compacts,
contractual agreements, and other established cooperative endeavors.*

The interstate library compact provides a legal base for extending
cooperative library services across state lines. Its enactment does not
establish such service, but it gives authority to state and local libraries
to do so. Under the compact, state libraries may make agreements to
provide services or permit the use of facilities on an interstate basis.

The compact should also authorize local libraries to make similar arrangements for providing services to residents of other states, and it should contain authority for all types of libraries to join in the provision of cooperative services. In the absence of a compact, contractual and other agreements should be explored.

5. *The state should gather, compile, interpret, publish, and disseminate annual statistics on all types of libraries in the state, including the state library agency. The state library agency should be a central information source concerning the libraries of the state.*

Statistics are a tool in state planning and development for which the state library agency has a direct responsibility. This responsibility and the requirement that libraries furnish pertinent information should be written into state law. It should be possible within every state to turn to state government for information about all library resources in the state including those of the state library agency. The annual information should be analyzed to determine trends and needs in library service, and should be distributed promptly to all libraries, library groups, and appropriate government offices as an aid in planning activities. Whenever possible, the gathering and tabulating of library statistics should be done in conjunction with other agencies of government which have data processing equipment.

6. *The annual statistics gathered by the individual states should be designed to provide a common core of data among the states and for the nation.*

To provide the information needed for research and library development at the local, state, and national levels, the state library agencies should collect and publish data comparable among the states. These data in turn will provide useful national information. The statistical programs should be coordinated with those of the U.S. Office of Education, which has responsibility for nationwide library data. Comparability can be obtained by using the definitions in *Library Statistics* and *USA Standard for Library Statistics.*[2]

7. *The state should also publish an annual report showing state library activity as a coordinating agency.*

Such a report will provide information about state-level services in

[2] Statistics Coordinating Project, *Library Statistics: A Handbook of Concepts, Definitions, and Terminology* (Chicago: American Library Assn., 1966); Council of National Library Associations, *USA Standard for Library Statistics* (New York: USA Standards Institute, 1969).

the promotion of library systems, consultation services, and distribution of state and federal aid.

8. *It is the responsibility and obligation of the state library agency to initiate and encourage research. A position including the duties of research and planning should appear in each state agency position roster.*

To fulfill its leadership role in statewide library planning and development, the state library agency should conduct or promote research programs, particularly in relation to national research needs, that identify the library resources and programs to meet the needs. Successful planning must be a continuous process and requires a continuous backup of reliable information to develop dependable guidelines for immediate and long-range library planning by the profession and for well documented justification before state legislatures and Congress for plans, programs, and budget requests.

9. *The state plan should indicate particularly the structure of coordinated library service needed to achieve national standards for all types of libraries.*

There are no specific structures of library service that apply equally in every state, but the essential ingredients are universal: local outlets for most frequent reading needs, regional resources of greater strength within practical reach of every resident, and access to specialized materials anywhere in the state. Whatever the structure, adequate, easy, prompt lines of communication and response should be provided.

10. *As a standard of first priority, every locality within the state should be encouraged to participate in a coordinated library system, so that every resident has access to the total library resources of the state.*

Only a few states have library service available to every resident. In all the other states, communities without facilities should receive prompt attention on the part of state library agencies. An overall coordinated structure is first necessary so that the unserved localities have a way to fit efficiently and economically into a coordinated system which makes better service possible. State development efforts should then be directed to the role of leadership in stimulating and guiding localities in the development of their facilities. Consultation, demonstration, and financial assistance are means that can be used for this purpose. Where local resources are inadequate to provide independent service, state agencies should encourage such devices as contractual arrangements or mergers.

11. *Some circumstances, such as very sparse population and low economic base in specific local areas, may lead the state to provide direct library service.*

Because no resident should be deprived of access to the record of knowledge, the state library agency should arrange service for areas without any local resources. As a minimum, this should provide for mail delivery of material specifically requested by individuals in the unserved districts. Bookmobile service may be used to provide library facilities in these areas. Provision of resources to unserved localities should be within a program which anticipates and encourages local support of service, and should not become a means which enables some localities to avoid local effort in support of libraries. In extreme circumstances of very sparse population, the state may need to provide service directly without any local or regional structure.

12. *A high-priority standard of library development is that of designating or developing a pattern of centers over the state so that everyone has access to more comprehensive resources and specialized staff in addition to the resources within his locality.*

The center is the unit to provide the level of library facilities specified in Standard 33. It may be any combination of resources capable of providing services over a wide area. The state library agency has responsibility for developing such higher levels of library resources over the state, and state funds will be necessary to bring them into existence. With this level of facility, readers would have access first to local collections for general reading, secondly to specialized resources through interlibrary loan, and then to a collection in some depth and to the guidance of specialized professional staff. Together the collection and the professional staff constitute essential ingredients of quality library service.

13. *The state library agency should make provision for reference, bibliographic, and interlibrary loan service to supplement community and regional libraries.*

In every state, information requests from any locality should be referred through area or regional centers up to and beyond the state level in order to draw upon the full resources of the nation. A statewide reference center should be maintained by the state library agency, either in connection with the state library collection (see Standards 30 and 31) and the state reference service (see Standard 43) or through contracts with other libraries within or outside the state. The stronger the local and regional facilities available to readers, the more specialized the state level reference and bibliographic service must become. State agencies should participate in and support interstate bibliographic centers, thus providing access to materials not held within the state.

14. *The state library agency must make provision for consultants sufficient in number to stimulate all libraries to develop their full potential. It is also advisable for qualified consultative services to be provided at a regional level.*

Consultation means individual or small-group contact of sufficient intimacy and duration to deal with specific needs and problems. All libraries need such guidance, not only those in an early state of development, but also the long-established libraries facing new pressures and problems, particularly the libraries in metropolitan areas affected by socioeconomic changes in urban-suburban development. The consultant can provide guidance on problems of concern to local personnel, assistance in identifying problems not clearly recognized and identification of opportunities for increased or improved service to specific age and interest groups (as children, young adults, adults, students, the elderly, and the retired). These workers help implement the statewide program set forth in the state plan (see Standard 2).

15. *State library consultant service should emphasize guidance in special aspects of library service.*

With the advent of new concepts involving systems of libraries, media centers, and consortia, consultant services will take on added dimensions in such specialized areas as automation, computer technology, cost analysis, and other aspects of administration.

The state library agency must recognize its responsible role for providing guidance in some special aspects of service as those to the disadvantaged, the handicapped, the institutionalized, and persons in business, industry, the professions, and government. It should coordinate, wherever appropriate, these consultant services with those provided at other levels in order to eliminate unnecessary duplication of expense and effort.

16. *The state library agency is responsible for interpreting library service to the government and to the public, and for promoting a climate of public opinion favorable to library development.*

The potentialities of library service must be understood by the citizen and the legislator. The individual should recognize the ways in which a sound library program can be of service. The government official should be kept informed about the increasing and more specialized reading being done by both students and adults.

State library agencies should provide professional public relations leadership, either through their own staffs or by contract with public relations firms, to inform the entire public of the services and needs of the total library complex of the state.

CHAPTER II

THE STATE AND FINANCING LIBRARY PROGRAMS

As the level of government responsible for education, the state has a direct obligation for adequate financing of library service over the state. The cost of libraries should be shared by the state along with local units of government. The guiding principle behind state financial contributions to library service is that of ensuring adequate service for all residents of the state. The contribution of the state occurs in the form of resources used directly by citizens, consultant services, library centers, as well as direct financial aid.

17. *The state should share in the direct costs for library services and facilities.*

Libraries are part of the state educational system. They· serve students of a public service agency to provide adequate minimum service to its plements the services of the others. Physical facilities affect the ability of a public service agency to provide adequate minimum service to its users. It is important for all libraries to achieve minimum standards. Since the state has a responsibility to help meet the cost of a basic program of services and facilities, it should have and exercise the authority to coordinate development in an orderly fashion.

18. *The state plan should identify the levels of financial support and service which libraries of all types must achieve in order to participate in the state program and to receive state financial aid. State library agencies should be responsible for determining that levels or standards are achieved.*

All libraries participating in the statewide program must carry their share of the total load. The function of the state should not be conceived as making up for lack of effort or for poor organization. The standards to be achieved should be based on national standards, adapted to the conditions and state of development within individual states. The contribution of the state to local library service should be conditioned upon achievement of these standards. No library or library system should be approved by the state or receive state aid unless it shows promise of achieving minimum national standards. State library agencies should be empowered by law to set standards of performance which libraries must maintain in order to be entitled to receive state financial aid.

19. *Federal funds, together with local and state funds, are essential if adequate library service is to be provided. Federal funds should be a regular and continuing part of the financial support for library development.*

Federal funds administered by the state library agencies should be used to sponsor experimental projects for which, under ordinary circumstances, local or state funds might not be available; initiate projects which may demonstrate the advisability of certain patterns of services; and promote and advance coordinated plans for statewide library services. A combination of federal and state funds should be used to equalize library services at all levels in relation to need and financial ability to support services.

20. *State legal provisions should encourage fiscal responsibility for library service by governmental units below the state level and should not impose arbitrary restrictions, such as tax-rate limitations.*

State statutes should require financial participation in support of library service by local jurisdictions. The regulations covering distribution of state funds should specify the minimum financial effort required. Those appropriating bodies which choose to provide greater funds for library service should not be restricted from doing so by a maximum tax rate or other limitation imposed by the state; it is the function of the state to ensure adequate service but not to limit it.

21. *State financial aid for libraries should equalize resources and services across the state by providing extra help for those least able to finance sound services and facilities.*

Once a minimum standard for the cost of library service is established, the portion to be provided by localities and the portion to be provided by the state and the federal government should be set. The state share may well be greater for those localities where a reasonable financial effort will not provide the local portion; in these cases the state equalizes resources. Areas requiring special help may be remote districts with very sparse population, governmental units with limited resources, and areas in transition. The assistance may take the form of direct grants and/or services provided by the state.

22. *Direct financial grants to local libraries should be conditional on the meeting of minimum standards of organization, qualifications of professional personnel, and financial effort for library support on the part of the governmental unit or appropriating body.*

Grants should not be made to libraries which cannot make effective use of them because of inadequate organization, personnel, or financial effort. Libraries receiving direct state aid should be organized within the statewide plan of service and participate in it. The level of financial support and of personnel to be achieved should be specified in state regulations and based upon conditions within the various states, with the national standards serving as a guide.

23. *Direct state aid should be granted to libraries not achieving minimum standards only if they formally agree to achieve standards within a specified time, and submit a plan for this purpose.*

One purpose of state library activity is to help weak libraries achieve adequacy; financial help can speed up the process. Care should be taken to be sure that such aid does not perpetuate library units which have no prospect of progressing to the point where people can get needed service and where state funds will ensure this goal. If state aid is granted to substandard libraries for an interim period, they must have a reasonable plan for achieving standards within a few years.

24. *State financial assistance should be provided to help meet the substantial costs involved in organizing or reorganizing library units into adequate systems and networks.*

Consistent with the underlying principle of state financial aid to libraries is the use of state funds to help bring about the statewide system of adequate library units. Such money may be used for demonstration grants to show what sound organization would provide, as establishment grants for new units which achieve or will shortly achieve state standards, or as short-term expansion grants for existing libraries which are prepared to take on greater responsibilities in accordance with the state's library development plan. The special funds may be used for any appropriate purpose commensurate with enlarged responsibilities; e.g., to build collections, to expand building space, to employ personnel, and to procure equipment or bookmobiles.

25. *State financial assistance should be provided to strong libraries which as resource centers for systems make available their resources and the services of their specialized personnel to the residents of a region.*

Every effort should be made to build on strengths of existing libraries rather than duplicating what already exists. The strength of these libraries should be used in any coordinated program of statewide library service. There should be provision for adequate remuneration of those libraries agreeing to enlarged responsibilities as an integral part of a statewide plan of library service.

26. *A determined portion of state financial assistance should be provided to libraries in metropolitan or other areas where there is evidence that their specialized staff, their resources in print and nonprint materials, and their services are used extensively by nonconstituents.*

State financial assistance should be sufficient to absorb the costs of library service to nonconstituents, and render unnecessary a charge for borrowers' cards. The state library agency should determine which libraries are eligible for such state aid. Local support of other libraries in the area should not diminish because of state aid to these strong libraries.

CHAPTER III

STATEWIDE DEVELOPMENT OF RESOURCES

The total library and information resources of the state must be developed, strengthened, and coordinated as a whole. On this foundation there can be built a strong structure of library services to individuals, societal groups, and government agencies. The speed and accuracy with which all the library and information resources within a state are made accessible for user needs are determined by the degree of success achieved in mobilizing the state's total subject and reference resources in an information network. Resources will be under-used when relationships between the various types of libraries are informal and loosely structured. To this end, the state library agency should (1) assist in the definition of roles, (2) assess strengths and weaknesses, and (3) foster formal cooperative agreements to make certain that full library services and total library and information resources are accessible to meet all user needs.

27. *Each state should have a comprehensive, long-range plan for developing, coordinating, maintaining, and improving the total library resources which affect the socioeconomic, political, cultural, intellectual, and educational life of the state.*

The full resources needed for affairs of state in this age encompass several million volumes. The holdings of state library agencies form one part of this total resource. Collections of public libraries; of schools; of colleges, universities, and institutions; and of private holdings in research and industrial centers are important additional portions. State library agencies should assume a leadership role in participation with other librarians and library interests in developing and coordinating the plan for building and using the total library resources within the state. Statewide planning should be conceived as a continuous program of goal-setting and evaluation rather than a one-time activity. Interstate compacts should be undertaken for joint acquisition of resources which would be available to all members of the compact.

28. *The informational resources within or accessible to each state should include, in addition to books, other printed materials in original or miniaturized form, and nonprint materials of all kinds.*

The knowledge needed in the affairs of state is contained as much in current journals, newspapers, reports, and other media as in books. Each state should be responsible for acquiring, organizing, storing, and developing means of rapid information retrieval of these many graphic records. Access to them is essential for the researcher, for the legislator, for the student, as well as for all other citizens.

29. *The state through its state library agency should exercise leadership in maintaining freedom to read and freedom of access to materials presenting varying views on controversial issues.*

People must have access to the full range of political, social, and religious viewpoints, in agencies of all sizes from the smallest library to the state library collection. Efforts of censors seeking to limit freedom to read should be resisted. It is incumbent upon the state library agency to see that legal channels are used if necessary and to help prevent censorship of materials whether in academic, public, or school libraries. The basic policies which should control access to resources reflecting various views are set forth in "The Freedom to Read" statement and the "Library Bill of Rights."[3]

30. *An important component in statewide resources should be a general collection of sufficient size and scope to supplement and reinforce resources of other libraries.*

The size and scope of the general collection should relate to other resources, both within and outside government. The holdings of existing libraries may be used to backstop the resources of both local and regional libraries. Resources available through interstate compacts may be needed to meet this standard. The state should share in the financing of the facilities on which it depends.

31. *The state should maintain in its comprehensive collection current information on present and potential public policies and state responsibilities as an important component of statewide resources.*

This collection serves government directly. It is also a vital resource for the enlightenment of the electorate. Therefore, it should be made widely and readily available.

32. *The library resources in state agencies and the wider resources in libraries associated in cooperative agreements should be widely and genuinely available through the following means: (1) central records of holdings, (2) bibliographies and indexes of state materials, (3) rapid communication systems among libraries to facilitate location of needed information and resources, (4) interlibrary loan provisions to the extent consistent with the need for material in the holding library, and (5) duplication equipment for supplying copies of material that cannot be loaned.*

There is no real value in building high-level subject and reference resources jointly in the major libraries of the state and then having them unknown or unavailable, so that the government officer, for example,

[3]"The Freedom to Read" statement was prepared by the Westchester Conference of the American Library Association and the American Book Publishers Council, 1953; the "Library Bill of Rights" was adopted by the Council of the American Library Association in 1948, revised in 1961, and further revised in 1967.

is unable to obtain what he needs when a given problem is before the state. State library collections, holdings in large municipal libraries, college and university collections, and even private research facilities should be included in this information network. Library resources for government and for the state in general must not only be acquired but must be mobilized for use.

33. *Subject and reference resources should also be available at regional centers within the state, at a distance which enables any serious reader to reach such facilities within a reasonable length of time.*

Normally these regional centers would be existing libraries, which broaden their usual resources and service area as they take on regional responsibilities. They should have state financial assistance to meet their regional obligations. If suitable agencies do not exist, the state should provide branches of the state library for the purpose. These regional centers should be part of the state network of library facilities, and in some cases might maintain special collections for the whole state on subjects of particular regional importance.

34. *The total resources in each state should include collections of audio-visual and of other new forms of communication media, which should be made available to users throughout the state.*

Films, filmstrips, slides, and recordings constitute valuable educational material for schools, organizations, and individuals. Newer forms of communication, such as microreproductions and programmed instructional materials, have assumed great importance. Plans for their coordinated provision should be developed, such as state centers, cooperative pools and circuits, and affiliates of regional libraries. Whatever the form of organization, the state has responsibility for reviewing the situation, promoting suitable facilities, and sharing in their cost. State library agencies should take the initiative in developing audio-visual and other programs.

35. *Resources available within or near each state should include a full range of reading materials for the blind and handicapped.*

Talking books on discs and tapes and books in braille are made available from the Library of Congress through regional centers. Books in large print should be purchased for the visually handicapped and captioned films made available for the deaf. The state is responsible for services which achieve the level set forth in *Standards for Library*

Services for the Blind and Visually Handicapped,[4] including publicizing the availability of such resources and promoting their use for the blind and other handicapped people. Working through appropriate agencies and institutions and professional personnel in contact with such persons, the state should identify the blind and other handicapped eligible and guide them in the use of these services. Responsibility extends to financial contribution by the state if these special resources are administered by a nonstate agency.

36. *Provision of storage for little-used materials, in concert with other libraries, is a vital part of the state's responsibility to maintain access to rare or out-of-print materials.*

Infrequently used materials tend to accumulate on the shelves of all libraries. Individual libraries hesitate to dispose of them because they may have some value. There should be within each state one or more centers to which such materials can be sent, one copy of which will be held if some future use is likely. This may be a storage unit within the state library or within centers elsewhere for which the state shares the cost.

CHAPTER IV

THE STATE AND INFORMATION NETWORKS

Public libraries have charted new courses in library development through establishment of the system concept; school systems are organizing their libraries into coordinated media programs; and in academic circles a definite trend is evident in the establishment of consortia. A new direction in library service, therefore, becomes clear. These groupings of libraries must be linked in a defined relationship with each other and with other information services to form "networks of knowledge."

A system is an association of similar types of organizations working together. A network is a combination of diverse information sources, linked in a formal relationship.

The role of the state library agency thus takes on added significance

[4] Commission on Standards and Accreditation of Services for the Blind, Committee on Standards for Library Services, *Standards for Library Services for the Blind and Visually Handicapped* (Chicago: American Library Assn., 1967).

in its responsibility to lead, coordinate, and guide these groups of libraries and other information sources into meaningful participation in such networks. The state library agency should employ financial incentives to this end (see Standard 24).

37. *The state library agency has a responsibility to promote the network concept for the optimum use of resources.*

The network ensures maximum use of the full range of both print and nonprint media and realia.

A formal, coordinated structure is essential to ensure maximum bibliographical access as well as effective and efficient utilization of the total library and information resources within a state. Only with a formal structure will the total library and information resources within a state be identified and enabled to function as components in the evolving national information systems.

38. *The state library agency must exercise leadership in determining the most advanced techniques in acquiring, recording, and processing all kinds of informational materials related to the special needs of the state, made accessible through networks.*

Networks will be effective only if the organization of materials at each level is based upon sound principles. The state library agency has a responsibility to advance technical services through centralized facilities, to achieve economical, expeditious ordering and processing of materials, and to assure a consistent quality of bibliographical data to provide orderly and ready retrieval of information and materials.

Through technology and technical competence, bibliographical access and exchange should be achieved, in order to draw universally upon "reservoirs of information."

39. *The state library agency should exert leadership to effect exchange of information and materials through networks that open new sources and channels for the flow of information.*

New methods of indexing, recording, storing, retrieving, and disseminating information are being developed by public and private agencies, frequently utilizing computers and other electronic devices.

The means and methods of assuring efficient access to information and materials will vary as each state develops the best possible pattern suited to its particular characteristics and resources.

40. *The state library agency has the responsibility for ensuring that the networks of library and information sources within the state's own borders transcend state boundaries and are linked to other networks—state, regional, national, and international.*

41. *The state has a responsibility to encourage by grants and other funding the development and continuation of networks.*

A combination of state and federal funds should be used to encourage the interrelationships of libraries, information centers, and bibliographic sources of all types and at all levels.

The state should make available to institutions, which enter into a formal network structure, financial compensation as an incentive to realize the full service potential.

CHAPTER V

LIBRARY SERVICES TO STATE GOVERNMENT

Relevant information and recorded knowledge must be continually brought to bear on the affairs of government. Lacking such resources, everyone from the chief executive to the individual state employee acts in at least partial ignorance. With these resources the legislator can know the facts in the case, the judge can trace the law that applies, and the department chief can be informed on the issues before him.

The general and the legal collections at the state level form the basis of library service to government. Indeed, reference and research resources over the state are called on as needed to meet state problems. In addition, the work of state government may require specialized collections and staff to support the functions of the judicial, legislative, executive, and administrative branches and of the special study commissions set up from time to time.

While many of the collections of materials—on law, documents, history, and archives—are vital to agencies and people outside state government, they are included here because no state government can function effectively without them.

42. *Each state should maintain a complete collection of the documents of its own government and of current documents of comparable states, plus a strong collection of both local and federal documents.*

Collections of government documents are of prime importance for historical research, public affairs, and for meeting particular informational needs. The full collection for each state would normally be maintained by the state library agency, and a checklist of state documents should be published periodically by the state. Regional centers for state documents should also be developed within the state in existing libraries, and the agencies administering them should be encouraged to collect local publications and official reports for their areas as well. The state should ensure that complete federal documents resources are universally available by endorsing the designation of strategically located federal regional depositories. These should be adequately organized, staffed, and serviced. The state may assist in funding to fulfill the functions stipulated in the Federal Depository Act of 1962.

43. *A high level of information and reference service for government agencies, courts, and studies must be maintained by the state.*

This begins with quick information service available both in person and by telephone. It extends to extensive bibliographic searches sometimes needed by officers and staff of government. It includes guidance and assistance to state researchers on government assignments. It may include précis writing and preparation of material for reports. Information service at the state level should reflect both reference skill and knowledge of public affairs and government. The information service is based upon the comprehensive collection maintained by the state, usually designated as the State Library. In those instances where another library or agency is available to serve the state government, the reference service must be conveniently and genuinely available to government workers during all hours when the offices are open.

44. *Special information and research service should be available to the legislative branch of government and provided as part of or in close coordination with state library agencies.*

This is often known as legislative reference or information service. It also involves research and the digesting of information, in a close and confidential relationship with members of the legislature. In some states this service is given by existing state library agencies, while in others a separate unit has developed. Where the legislative agency is a separate unit, the state library should assure that the necessary back-up collections are readily available and accessible. So important is basing action at the state level on facts that this facility should be well developed in every state with specialized staff assigned specifically to work with the legislature. Legislative reference service is one of the important resources specified by the Council of State Governments: "To meet their generally increased responsibilities, the state legislatures need the assistance of highly competent service and research staffs."[5]

45. *Each state should maintain a law collection covering the complete body of primary and secondary legal materials, in order to provide the best possible legal resources for the operation of state government and for the administration of justice.*

The size and depth of the collection depend upon the proximity of the law library to other and more comprehensive legal collections. The collection should contain the complete primary and secondary materials of the state itself. These include constitutions, codes and statutes, session laws and other legislative documents and materials, court reports and court rules (high, intermediate, and special courts), appellate court records and briefs, opinions of the attorney general, decisions and rules and regulations of administrative agencies and tribunals, digests and encyclopedias, citators, indexes, local treatises and practice books, publications of the law schools and bar associations, and primary materials of the local government corporations. There should be duplication of the state materials, since the law library should serve as a repository therefor.

The same categories of materials should be held for all other states, with the possible exception of local treatises and practice books, digests, legislative history materials, records and briefs, and local materials below the state level. The primary and secondary legal materials of the federal government are essential, including the reports (decisions) of all federal courts and administrative agencies, statutory materials and legislative histories, treaties, administrative rules and regulations, digests, and citators. The location of the law collection in relation to the comprehensive general state library will determine the need for the nonlegal state and United States government documents and for other nonlegal but related materials.

There should be complete coverage of the regional reporter system (reports and citators), the American digest system, annotated and selected subject reports and digests, treatises and related materials, looseleaf services, restatements of the law, uniform state laws, legal periodicals and the indexes thereto, American Bar Association publications,

---

[5] Committee on Organization of Legislative Services of the National Legislative Conference, *Mr. President . . . Mr. Speaker* (Chicago: Council of State Governments, 1963), p.9.

annual institutes, dictionaries, form books, bibliographies and bibliographic tools, as well as a strong collection of the literature related to the law. Primary and selected secondary legal materials for the principal Anglo-American jurisdictions are necessary. The extent of the collection of international and comparative law and of foreign law will depend upon the circumstances of need and use as well as upon the location of the law library with respect to a more comprehensive legal collection in the area.

The law collection should be maintained for the judicial, legislative, and executive branches of state government and for the lower courts, attorneys, students, and the general public. If the appellate court and executive departments operate outside the state capital, branch legal collections must be maintained in these locations. The law collection should serve as a resource center for the libraries of the circuit or county courts and the bar associations.

46. *A strong collection of history related to the state—regional, state, and local—should exist where it is accessible to government officials, research workers, and the interested public.*

It should be possible in every state to go to one collection, or to two or more closely coordinated collections, where the primary, nonofficial source materials relating to the history of the state are preserved and available. These source materials would include private manuscripts, corporate records, files of locally published newspapers, periodicals, pamphlets, maps, broadsides, photographs, and publications relating to the history of the area and its people. State historical agencies have traditionally assumed the responsibility for collecting these materials. However, where existing collections are incomplete, inadequate, or unavailable, the state should provide for collecting these materials. The purposes of this collection include both support of the intensive study of the state's political, economic, and cultural history and provision of background on current problems.[6]

47. *Each state should have an archival program for the preservation and organization of the state's own records and the records of local government, and should have a records management program for the retirement and disposition of nonessential state records.*

An archival depository is necessary to preserve and service perma-

[6] See Appendix 1, "State and Local History. . . ."

nently valuable official records needed for the legal and administrative functioning of government, for the verification and protection of the rights of individuals, and for historical and other research. It should include the records of antecedent colonial and territorial governments. The materials should not only be stored, but also be arranged and described so that needed records can be found readily. Unless the head of the archival agency is also in charge of records management in the agencies and subdivisions of the state, he should have close working arrangements with the agency or agencies that exercise this function. Inasmuch as he has basic responsibility for the selection and preservation of permanently valuable records, no records should be destroyed without his approval. In states where responsibility for local archives rests with local governments, it is the task of the state archival agency to stimulate interest in their preservation and to furnish guidance in the application of proper methods.

48. *Specialized working libraries may be needed in some divisions and agencies of government, and should be developed as branches of or in close coordination with the central library agency which has the comprehensive collection.*

Individual officers and workers often need ready reference sources located immediately at hand. With a strong central collection and services available (see Standards 30, 43, and 45), these quick reference needs can be served by carefully selected desk collections or shelves of books in offices. If necessary, small working collections can be set up for this purpose without establishing complete libraries. Where the size, location, and nature of the particular government department makes separate libraries essential, they should be planned and coordinated in close relation to the central library agency. Uniform systems for acquisition, processing, and discarding should be followed, and a union list of materials should be maintained. The central library should act as backstop for departmental libraries while at the same time departmental library resources should be available for general use.

49. *A clear and continuing official relationship should exist between state library agencies and officials with responsibility for the libraries which the state maintains for its health, welfare, and correctional programs.*

This relationship facilitates both the initial development of institutional libraries and their continual guidance. The relationship should be set forth in official statements of policy so that it is recognized by institution and other government officials concerned (fiscal, personnel, etc.) as well as by state library officers. The standards to be maintained can be derived from official library standards for health care facilities, school media programs, and correctional institutions and adjusted to the specific purposes of each agency.

50. *The library programs maintained in state institutions should be an integral part of their treatment and rehabilitation programs.*

The institutional library has an influential role to play in the rehabilitation process, and should provide carefully selected materials which contribute to educational, vocational, recreational, and cultural programs. The collection should be geared to the special reading needs and abilities of the institutional residents.

Bibliotherapy should be developed and utilized in the rehabilitation process. Institutions should provide access to legal materials for residents who seek better understanding of their civil status.

Qualified staff in institutional libraries should participate in staff meetings and in the development of rehabilitation programs.[7]

51. *The resources of state institutional libraries should meet the immediate administrative and technical needs of the staff, and should be tied into networks of resources for specialized materials not held within the institutions.*

Since staffs of institutions are specialized in training and skill, resources at their command should include good working collections, whether in medical, welfare, or correctional fields. Institutional library collections, as well as other decentralized departmental collections maintained by the state, should be tied into networks of resources for specialized materials. Particular attention must be given to rapid communication between the state library and all institutional libraries.

CHAPTER VI

ORGANIZATION OF STATE LIBRARY SERVICES

There is no one standard structure or prototype for state library service. State governments have developed in different ways,

[7] See also Appendix 2, "The Relationship and Responsibilities of the State Library Agency to State Institutions."

at different times, and to different extents. Historical growth has played a part in state library organization, as have principles of administration applied to the structure of state government.

A state library agency carries the major responsibility for library development and library coordination. It is that unit in state government charged by law with providing the state's library program, with coordinating library planning for total library service, and, in many cases, serving state government.

It receives and disburses state and federal funds for library services according to state and federal authorizations and appropriations. It is responsible for the statewide library program: for research, planning, leading, and coordinating; for seeing that services improve and development takes place within the state; for providing direct services where appropriate; and for acting on behalf of the state in cooperative programs with agencies outside the state.

The administrative structure for library service need not be the same from state to state, even as it need not be the same among private enterprises. There are, however, principles of organization which apply generally, and which must be followed if the full range of state library activities is to be maintained at a sound level and at reasonable cost. These principles form the basis of the standards for state library organization.

52. *The agency or agencies providing state library services should rest upon clear statutory provisions which define the functions to be performed, provide authority for these activities, and ensure the legal basis for a flexible program to meet the needs of the state.*

Because library agencies have developed over a period of time and in different ways, agencies sometimes rest upon an ambiguous legal foundation. Their authority should be clarified and made explicit by statute. It should be possible in every state to find the legal authorization for the program maintained. This authority should not be narrow or restrictive, but rather should provide opportunity for meeting library needs as they emerge.

53. *The state library or state library agencies should be so placed in the structure of government that they have the authority and status to discharge their responsibilities.*

State library functions are best constituted as a separate agency of state government, directly responsible through its chief administrator or its governing board to the executive and legislative branches of government. A governing board of lay citizens, comparable in power to local library boards and boards of education, sometimes functions to develop a vital library program. Such a group should be appointed by the governor or other elected official who is visible to the electorate and responsive to its needs. The library agency or agencies should not be subject to political pressures or to changes in personnel and policy at each election.

The organization of state government sometimes calls for combining related activities within a comprehensive department, which may result in placing of library agencies in a more inclusive division, such as a department of education. This in itself does not necessarily restrict the library program. But if this organization prevails, library agencies should have the stature and autonomy within the larger unit to achieve their distinctive functions and to bring libraries up to standard. Administrative simplification is often the reason for placing a library function in a larger department, but this should not subordinate the planning and program functions of the library agency. If a comprehensive department of state government is not willing or able to give adequate status and support to the library division within it, the library functions should be transferred to a more compatible department or made independent under a lay board.

54. *Every state should make administrative provision for the following major areas of state library service: providing, correlating, and servicing print and nonprint resources; giving direct service to state government; planning and coordinating total library service; and supervising state and federally funded programs. Qualified personnel must be assigned to each area.*

It should be possible in each state to identify these several functions and the personnel responsible for them. The functions may or may not be within one state library organization. If two or more areas of library service are combined in one administrative division, each should be provided to the extent necessary in the state and one should not be neglected in favor of the other. No matter what the variations, it should be possible to identify the responsible units and to verify that the units recognize and discharge their obligations.

55. *The several state library agencies dealing with the broad areas of state responsibility should be unified as one department or division of govern-*

ment to the extent possible and advisable under state law, policy, and tradition.

Reorganization need not be forced if the full state program is coming up to standards, but equally it should not be delayed because of inertia. Even as the state's responsibilities for schools are best handled in a single education department, so the library affairs of the state should be administratively unified. This unification enhances planning for full library needs, balanced development among library functions, coordination among related activities, effective overall budget preparation and presentation, and efficient use of facilities, as well as the avoidance of unnecessary duplication. Most important, a unified state library agency permits the strongest leadership at the state level. Unification does not mean subjection or neglect of particular functions; Standard 54 specifies that each function must have identity and qualified personnel. Every state, and every state library official, has an obligation to plan for an orderly development of library services toward coordination of library activities in a structure which provides status and a proper place for all library functions maintained by the state.

56. *Provision should be made in every state for agencies or units devoted to such special services as historical materials, law collections, archival materials, and legislative information and research service.*

These special services have developed in various structures in the states: sometimes as part of a central state library agency, sometimes in separate units, sometimes as independent agencies. Historical collections, for example, have been built by state historical societies and groups; many law collections are under the jurisdiction of supreme courts; archival resources are closely associated with the record-keeping function of government and therefore are related to the department or division of administration; legislative information service may be an arm of the legislature. Each of these may operate effectively as integral parts of a central library organization, or as units of government which they serve, or as independent agencies. In any case, adequate provision must be made for these important services. Whatever the organizational structure, such special services should be coordinated with other state library resources and services, as provided in Standard 57.

57. *To the extent that library agencies remain separate entities at state level, they should be coordinated in a clear-cut plan which provides for con-*

sultation and cooperation and which specifies division of responsibility.

A special obligation for joint planning and for coordinated development falls upon the administrators of separate state library agencies. Cordial relations alone are not enough. The functions of each agency should be defined and recorded; activities not covered should be allotted to a designated unit; unnecessary duplication of resources or staff should be eliminated; facilities should be shared wherever possible; and the whole state library program should proceed as an entity even though provided by different administrative units. Included in this need for coordination are facilities, resources, and technical services for research and specialized workers, for students of all ages, and for general readers—children, young adults, and adults.

58. *Advising and supervising school media centers should be an accepted state responsibility.*

The school library is a multimedia center and must be an integral part of the total school program. For this reason, media consultants at the state level should be in the closest possible organizational contact with other consultants and supervisors responsible for the curricula and special aspects of elementary and secondary schools. Such integration is usually best achieved by placing the functions of media specialists (library and audio-visual specialists) in the Department of Education. The Council of Chief State School Officers has issued a clear statement of *Responsibilities of State Departments of Education for School Library Services.*[8]

Consultant service to media centers must be closely coordinated with other state library activities because of the expanding demands for library materials by students and in the interest of coordination at the state, regional, and local level. Coordination can be accomplished by frequent and meaningful contact between the state library agency director and the chief state school officer and through a school–public library liaison officer.

59. *The state library agency should function as a coordinating and service agency to expedite the cooperative programs of academic, special, school, and public libraries in the same community, region, state, and nation; to strengthen the total resources and services available to library*

[8] Council of Chief State School Officers, *Responsibilities of State Departments of Education for School Library Services* (Washington, D.C.: The Council, 1961).

users; and to enable library support to achieve the maximum benefit through the coordinated effort of participating libraries.

The system concept of library service has as much application to academic, special, and school libraries as to public libraries. In view of the increasing interdependence of all types of libraries, it becomes increasingly important to eliminate duplication of effort and expense. The library agency at the state level is in a unique position to serve the coordinating function which is required to bring all of the programs of library service into meaningful focus.

60. *State library agencies should function in close contact with library groups and citizens throughout the state.*

As service agencies, state library units must avoid isolation from the people they serve. Effective working contacts should be maintained with related organizations in the state. The state librarian or other library officer must participate in the deliberations or activities of such associations. If the state library agency is not governed by a lay board, an advisory group to work with state library officials should be established. Such an advisory council can lend substantial assistance and leadership to state library agencies and to the general development of library service. Close contact with library and citizen interests throughout the state will ensure a program in tune with the needs of the people served.

CHAPTER VII

PERSONNEL

Recognized principles of personnel management apply to all library personnel employed at the state level. In addition, the qualifications for the performance of state agency personnel must be higher because of the leadership, consultative, and planning responsibilities which require extensive and varied professional experience, maturity of judgment, imagination, and demonstrated management ability.

The essential theme underlying these standards for state library service is that state library agencies must exercise leadership. It grows out of both the responsibilities and the opportunities of library service at the state level. Leadership and top quality service will not be possible unless the very best librarians are attracted to state service.

The state library personnel may render both general and special library service, and may be responsible for both popular and research resources. Special qualifications and experience are required in such areas of responsibility as law, legislative reference, public relations, subject bibliography, data processing, systems management, planning and equipping library buildings, and services to special groups.

61. *State library agency personnel should meet the highest professional standards, in addition to the requirements for special positions involved in state service. The distinctive quality of the effective librarian—sound judgment in adjusting library service to meet a variety of needs and ability to work with a variety of people—should be particularly in evidence.*

Each member of the professional library staff should hold a degree from a graduate library school accredited by the American Library Association or by the accrediting authority of the state. Other professional staff should have education pertinent to their responsibilities. Consultants should have background and experience in the type of library service on which they consult. Specialists for law, history, legislative reference, and other disciplines should be required to have advanced study in the subject fields with which they deal. The professional requirements for library personnel at the state level should be competitive on a national basis to enable the state to lead the way in building quality staffs.

62. *Appointment to state library employment should be for merit alone, and dismissal should occur only for incompetence or grave personal cause.*

Party affiliation or political contribution should not be a factor in appointment or dismissal of state library personnel, including the administrator of the agency, and political endorsements should not be required for selection. Selection is best determined by unassembled competitive examination, involving an objective review of candidates' academic and job performance and personal qualifications. Appointment should be on tenure after an initial probationary period. Dismissal should occur only after the presentation of charges against the employee, which he should have an opportunity to answer and, if he wishes, have examined by a reviewing panel. All state library positions should be under a sound personnel program providing tenure.

63. *All employees of state library agencies should work within a position classification plan which provides for defined levels of employment, to*

the end that the agency's service responsibilities may be conducted with efficiency and economy.

The personnel of a state library agency is composed of three levels of staff—professional, para- or subprofessional, and clerical—with differing educational backgrounds. The professional performs administrative, consultative, and service duties (either those of librarianship or of other disciplines) with only general supervision. One level of para- or subprofessional is assigned limited professional tasks under direct supervision of a qualified professional. An employee in this level should be a college graduate with knowledge and skills adapted to his work assignment. An employee in another level of para- or subprofessional staff may be a graduate of a junior or community college, or possess a technical education beyond that of high school. He may be assigned clerical duties of a complex nature or a simple supervisory responsibility under the general guidance of a professional librarian. The clerical employee, who should be a high school graduate with training suited to his work, performs a variety of assigned tasks under sufficient supervision to ensure satisfactory performance. There should be an adequate number of the para- or subprofessional and clerical employees to free the professional staff for duties and responsibilities which require their specialized skills.

All positions at whatever level should be classified so that each employee works at his highest level of competence and develops his experience and job knowledge to compete for more responsible and remunerative positions.

64. *Employment within a state library program should constitute a career service which provides genuine opportunity for advancement.*

The career structure should rest upon a classification and pay plan which clearly defines the several kinds and levels of employment and salaries for them. Merit increases in salary should be provided, so that each appointee can anticipate increases in salary if his performance comes up to established standards and as he gains competence in his job.

Opportunities for promotion from one level to another should be provided. Where advancement requires additional education or formal training, staff should be encouraged to qualify through provision of scholarships, leaves with pay, sabbatical leaves, payment of tuition, and the like.

65. *Professional positions in the state library service should be open to all qualified candidates.*

For the good of the state, it should be able to draw on the professional personnel of the nation as vacancies occur. Knowledge of the individual state and service experience in it are desirable but not essential. Loyalty to the state served is essential on the part of every state worker, and, given this condition, the professional can develop his knowledge of the state and its unique requirements.

66. *Appropriate salary provisions, related to defined levels of employment within the classification plan, should be provided. Opportunities for advancement should exist for those qualified to render high professional service. Administrative responsibilities should not be the only determining factor.*

Particular attention must be given to the middle range of salaries for persons with substantial professional but limited administrative responsibility, to be sure that compensation provides a satisfactory career for members of a learned profession. One significant measure in setting salaries for state library agency workers is the remuneration provided other professional workers in the state service with comparable amount of education and responsibility.

Salaries for professional personnel should be at or above the national level for positions requiring comparable ability, experience, and responsibility, as well as comparable to those in other state departments. Salaries for subprofessional personnel should be competitive with non-library positions in the state service.

67. *The conditions and perquisites of state library employment should be comparable to practices in the progressive libraries in the state and nation.*

A sound retirement program for which the state shares the cost should be open to all state library staff members. Annual vacation should be at least twenty working days, and some provisions for compensatory time should be provided for the extra hours often worked by field consultants and others. Health insurance should cover both regular and major medical expenses. Payment for sickness should be extensive enough to protect the employee during prolonged as well as occasional illness. These several provisions are designed to provide staff members a sense of security and thus enable them to give full attention and energy to the service of the state. The state should permit and encourage state library staff members to attend professional meetings, should grant leaves for advanced study, and should contribute toward the costs of such continuing professional education.

68. *The state library agency has responsibility for helping to develop ade-*

*quate library personnel resources in the state by means of recruitment
to the profession, provision of placement services to libraries and librarians, and full utilization of human resources.*

The state has the first obligation for education for librarianship within its borders. This responsibility starts with the development of strong,
professional library schools, either within the state or within reach of
state residents. State-financed scholarships for library education should
be available. A formal program of recruitment to the profession should
be established and every available means should be used for encouraging
state residents to enter the profession. The program of recruitment
should include attracting competent workers to the state. Placement
service for libraries and librarians should be made available. Once
librarians have accepted positions within the state, their full capacities should be utilized by providing the opportunities for transfer
and promotion within the state as need arises. A personnel inventory
for this purpose should be maintained at the state level. The state
library agency also has the responsibility for developing the leadership
potential in members of the profession within the state.

69. *The state library agency should promote and provide a program of continuing education for library personnel at all levels as well as for trustees.*

Rapidly changing conditions in library service, organizational patterns, and administration require continuing study by all library personnel. Even professionals in large library systems, including academic
institutions, may not be aware of the emerging library technology and
service potentialities or be prepared to use and promote them. Opportunities for keeping abreast of new developments in library service
should be provided to librarians, administrators, and trustees alike.

The state library agency must assume the responsibility for promoting and providing opportunities to achieve this goal by: (1) cooperat-
ing with library schools to provide institutes and other refresher courses,
(2) working with the officers and leaders in professional and other library associations and related groups to conduct meetings and seminars,
and (3) sponsoring meetings, seminars, and workshops for the continuing education of librarians and trustees.

70. *State governments should establish and enforce certification regulations
covering professional positions in publicly supported libraries and, to
the extent possible, privately supported libraries.*

Librarians render a professional service which must be kept at a high level. The public should be protected against unqualified personnel seeking to provide these services. Whenever public funds support any aspect of library service, certified staff should be required in order to ensure effective use of the money. Provisional certification may be granted for partially trained staff members, but only when full certification is planned within a few years. Certification of professional library personnel should be mandatory.

CHAPTER VIII

PHYSICAL FACILITIES FOR STATE LIBRARY SERVICES

State library services require facilities designed to accommodate their unique functions. Such buildings should meet the standards for other libraries, where applicable, be functional, flexible, and inviting.

71. *The program of library service determines the physical facilities.*

Planning or remodeling a library building, from its inception to its completion, should be undertaken by a team of experts. The team should include the governmental authority responsible for its construction, the librarian, the architect, and a library building consultant. Planning must start with a careful study of the needs and objectives of the library service program, a review of materials about library buildings and the planning of library buildings, and visits to existing libraries. The study should be followed by a written building program statement, prepared in consultation with staff members.

72. *Buildings to house state library services should be situated centrally to provide maximum accessibility to all components of state government which they serve.*

Service to government—the legislative, executive, and judicial branches—is a prime responsibility of state library agencies. Accessibility of resources to state legislators and their staff, to members of the executive departments and their staff, and to members of the judiciary and their staff is of vital importance to the ability of these servants of the state to perform adequately their tasks.

73. *A state library building should have all the qualities of a well-planned*

library plus the provision for space which its special functions require.

Archival and similar records, talking books, and books in braille require extra space and load-bearing capacities. Historical materials may require special vaults. Storage facilities are needed for little-used materials. The nature of use of the state collection calls for considerable study space for individuals, such as carrels.

In view of the confidential as well as advisory nature of the work of many staff members, individual offices should be provided. Adequate office space should be provided for supportive staff.

Multipurpose meeting rooms should be provided for the variety of activities and conferences carried on by state library agencies.

74. *An architect should be commissioned who combines the abilities to plan for functional needs and to design an aesthetically satisfying structure compatible with other state buildings.*

Not all architects have experience in designing library buildings. Often, the utilization of a state architect may be required. A well-prepared, detailed building program is a basic element toward assuring the design of a functional structure. The library building consultant member of the team working with the architect is another assurance. In some cases, it may be desirable to bring in consulting architects who have had experience with library buildings. It is essential that the architect work with all these advisers to guarantee that the functional needs of the library be met, and that it be attractive, inviting, and compatible with other state buildings.

75. *The site, plan, and construction of state library buildings should provide for maximum flexibility in the use of space. Programs and patterns of operation should not be limited by the building design. Expansion to meet future demands should be easy to achieve.*

Building for state library service must reflect the dynamic growth of library services. Needs will continually change and expand. Bearing walls must be kept at a minimum to permit reallocation of space when deemed necessary. It must be possible to adjust space to new needs and to add vertically or horizontally when necessary.

The future of all library service lies in diminishing compartmentalization and in achieving greater coordination of resources and services for the benefit of the user. The individual more and more will expect and demand easy access to all libraries. Only those institutions flexible enough to respond to such demands will survive; others inevitably will be replaced by new structures designed to perform the needed functions. Eventually, as the concept of service unimpeded by institutional barriers gains acceptance, standards for all types of libraries may be developed jointly, rather than each type for itself.

Standards for Library Functions at the State Level makes certain requirements of any agency authorized to provide library-related services throughout the province or state, regardless of the different institutional patterns which may have developed. The very diversity of structure among state library agencies has compelled an emphasis on *functions* to be performed for the *user*, who thus becomes the central figure he should be. In consequence, the stress which might otherwise have been laid on the institution itself is minimized in these standards.

The flexibility forced upon the state library agency by its own diversity, reinforced by its responsibility for statewide coordination and planning, impels it to lead in the transition from institution-centered librarianshp to user-oriented service.

STATE AND LOCAL HISTORY:
THE STATE'S RESPONSIBILITY FOR COLLECTION
AND CARE

The state has a responsibility to preserve its history and its historical resources. It is the duty of the state to collect material bearing upon the history of the state and of the territory therein, to make the material available to the public and to preserve it for future generations. The state's historical collection should include information on the political, religious, economic, and cultural history of the state and area. It is important not only that the state's historical background be stressed, but that the collection be kept alive and up-to-date and include information, historical and statistical, relative to the present time. Materials in the state's historical collection should include printed histories—regional, state, and local; maps of the state and territory; pamphlets; broadsides; programs; pictures; files of newspapers published in the state; locally published periodicals; histories of business firms, organizations, schools; house organs; trade catalogs; sermons; speeches; biographies and biographical material about citizens of the state; books by state authors; private manuscripts.

CUSTODY OF MATERIALS

While these materials are diverse in their characteristics, they may be placed in the charge of a single state agency, if facilities for the proper housing and funds for the administration by professionally trained personnel are provided. In those states where there is no existing agency supported by state funds, such as a state historical society with state support, or where such an agency exists but is not actively engaged in collecting and making available resources connected with the state, it is the responsibility of the state library to assume these duties. The state should assume the task of collecting state and local history for all the people of the

Prepared for the Local and State History Committee by Mrs. Hazel W. Hopper, Head, Indiana Division, Indiana State Library, and approved by the Executive Board of the American Association of State Libraries, June 26, 1967.

state. The task should not be left entirely to private organizations whose main responsibilities are to the membership of their associations.

Private manuscripts such as letters, diaries, journals, account books of a nonpublic origin pertaining to the state and its people should be included in the state's historical collection. Inasmuch as the care, cataloging, and preservation of manuscripts involve different procedures and techniques than those of the librarian, the state should establish qualifications for the position of curator of manuscripts that includes special training in or knowledge of such techniques.

STATE DOCUMENTS

A state agency, preferably the state library, should be a central depository for its own state documents. It should be the agency to distribute its state documents to other libraries within the state and to document centers outside the state. Depository libraries should be designated throughout the state so that the people will have ready access to state publications. The central depository library or state agency responsible for collecting state documents should publish periodically a checklist of state publications, and if no checklist of earlier publications has been made, the depository library should oversee such a project, and keep the checklist up to date.

LEGAL PUBLICATIONS

A collection of session laws of the state, constitutions, codes, legislative reports and journals, court reports, opinions of the attorney general, and rules and regulations of the various departments should be on file for the use of the public. If the state law library is established strictly for use by the state courts, the agency responsible for the state and local history collection should acquire copies of those legal publications which are necessary in the field of historical research.

LOCAL RESOURCES

There should be a survey conducted on a state level to determine the holdings in the field of local history and the manuscript holdings of state interest of public and college libraries, museums, and historical societies within the state. The results of the survey should be kept on file in the state's historical collection, so that research students could be referred to the proper institution for materials in their fields of interest.

The staff of the agency responsible for the state's historical collection should act in an advisory capacity to the public libraries, museums, and local historical societies throughout the state on problems of organization and care of local history collections, as well as encourage such developments.

COORDINATION AND EXTENSION OF LOCAL COLLECTIONS

Bibliographies and lists of current books and pamphlets in the field of state and local history which would be of interest for local historical collections should be prepared. Having access to bibliographies and checklists that are not available to librarians of small libraries or curators of local museums or historical societies, the state agency should keep them informed of books or documents that have particular importance to their communities.

In states where there are several institutions collecting state and local history such as the state library and the state historical society, an attempt should be made to coordinate the collections so that the institutions do not compete with each other in the acquisition of materials.

ARCHIVES

An archival depository is necessary to preserve and service permanently valuable official records needed for the legal and administrative functions of state government, for the verification and protection of the rights of individuals, and for historical and other research. The care and custody of state archives must be fixed by law. It cannot be arbitrarily decided upon by any particular official or agency. Public records are public property and must remain in an unbroken line of custody. Consequently public records may not be removed from the office of origin except to go into the official archives. If the archival responsibility is assigned by law to the state library, the library is committed to an active program. If it is assigned to another state agency, the library should not attempt to duplicate this function. Materials in the archival depository should be arranged according to archival policies and in an orderly manner, so that needed records are readily accessible for research. Inasmuch as the state archivist has basic responsibility for selection and preservation of permanently valuable records, no records of any state department should be destroyed without his permission. This should be guaranteed by law.

In states where the responsibility of local archives rests with the local government, the state archivist should give guidance to the local government in the proper care of their records.

STAFF QUALIFICATIONS

Archival techniques and procedures are unique and the archives depository should be administered by a professional staff, especially trained or experienced in archival management.

The staff of the state's historical collection is responsible for the dispensing of knowledge on the history of the state, through the use of the collection in its care. The state should require that prerequisites for application for professional positions be a knowledge of the history and government of the state and training in library science.

THE RELATIONSHIP AND RESPONSIBILITIES
OF THE STATE LIBRARY AGENCY
TO STATE INSTITUTIONS

The provision of adequate library services to and within state institutions is of growing concern to state library agencies. This concern stems from several factors:

1. The increased recognition of the need for more fully developed programs of rehabilitation and education to serve the unique and individual needs of institutionalized persons whether in hospitals, correctional institutions or those for persons with special handicaps
2. The widening gap between the growing improvement of public, school, and college libraries, and the woeful inadequacy or nonexistence of library service in many institutions
3. The growing awareness, reflected in various federal legislation, of the responsibility of federal and state governments to improve the opportunities of disadvantaged persons (or persons with special needs) within society.

Persons in institutions, whether hospitals, correctional institutions, or residential schools for persons with special handicaps, have needs that are unique to the individual and/or the type of institution. Library services must be geared not only to general interests and abilities, but to the special needs of persons in various types of institutions and to the purpose and program of each institution. Some of these may require services, materials, and library programs that are highly specialized. The primary purpose of such library service can be determined only in terms of that of the institution.

Library services must also provide for the staff and residents in the institution. Each agency must fulfill its own responsibility for the basic services and collections which will be meaningful for staff, residents, patients, or inmates.

A Look at Standards

Standards exist which outline the scope of these responsibilities.

Standards for Library Functions at the State Level identifies three broad areas of state responsibility for library service:

1. Statewide library resources for both government and citizens
2. Library services for state government
3. Statewide library development.

In the chapter "Library Services to State Government," the following standards specifically mention state institutions:

> A clear and continuing official relationship should exist between state library agencies and officials with responsibility for the libraries which the state maintains for its health, welfare, and correctional programs. (Standard 49)

> The library programs maintained in state institutions should be an integral part of their treatment and rehabilitation programs. (Standard 50)

> The resources of state institutional libraries should meet the immediate administrative and technical needs of the staff, and should be tied into networks of resources for specialized materials not held within the institutions. (Standard 51)

A number of statements on the responsibility of the state library agency have relevance for institutional libraries as well as for all other types of library service:

1. The state resource center, with all types of materials and services to state government and citizens (Standards 13, 27, 30, 34, 35)
2. State library agency participation in leadership and planning, and initiation of planning groups for all types of library service within the state (Standards 1, 2, 10)
3. Coordination of library services (Standards 9, 10, 59)
4. Gathering and publishing statistics—and central information (Standards 5, 7).

Specific standards exist for libraries in hospitals, correctional institutions, schools, etc.[1] These standards place the administrative and fiscal responsibilities for library service within the institution itself and within the state agency of which it is a part. In addition, they point to the role of the state library agency as one of supplying supplementary resources and services and of coordinating a state-wide program.

[1] "Library Services" in *Manual of Correctional Standards* (3d ed.; New York: American Correctional Assn., 1966); *Standards for School Media Programs* (Chicago: American Library Assn., 1969; Washington, D.C.: National Education Assn., 1969); *Standards for Library Services in Health Care Institutions* (Chicago: A.L.A., forthcoming).

The public library standards indicate that public libraries have a role to play in providing service to individuals and groups with special needs.[2]

FUNCTIONS AND RESPONSIBILITY

1. *The state library agency*
   a. Stimulation and initiation of studies, plans, and recommendations leading to improving library service
   b. Coordination of existing resources and services to strengthen institutional library service
   c. Technical professional advice and assistance on a continuing, consistent basis
   d. Coordinating the library needs and efforts of other agencies within the state into coordinated program and state plan
   e. Providing supplementary resources and reference services
   f. Collecting and disseminating statistics and information on status of libraries.

2. *The state agency or department responsible for the administration of the institutions*
   a. Development of a comprehensive plan for an effective program of library services
   b. Provision for implementation of such policies
   c. Provision for agency-level professional direction, supervision, and evaluation of library services at all institutions under agency jurisdiction
   d. Provision for adequate financial support for libraries
   e. Coordination of library program with total state library efforts and those of other agencies.

3. *Individual institutions*
   a. Administration and operation of library service in accordance with needs of the institution
   b. Development of policies and procedures for utilization of collections and services of other libraries to supplement library collections.

Since few institutions can maintain collections, personnel, and other resources to meet all needs, provisions must be made for supplementary resources from outside. Both the state department responsible for the administration of the institution and the state library agency have responsibilities for supplementing and improving local institution services.

The major and unique role of the state library agency should be to assist each agency to carry out its own role in a coordinated effort. The de-

[2]*Minimum Standards for Public Library Systems, 1966* (Chicago: American Library Assn., 1967).

velopment of state plans and the plans and policies of each appropriate agency and institution should reflect this purpose. The state library agency, in administering federal funds and other appropriations, should strengthen the capability of each agency to carry out its own share of the program.

It is realized that all state departments and their institutions are not capable of or ready to assume their full share of responsibility of providing for library services. However, the long-term goals of library development in institutions can be achieved only when each agency is able to carry out its own function and, at the same time, to become a part of the coordinated effort toward a viable network of library services.

Whenever, for reasons of practical expediency or other purposes, the state library agency, a public library, or other institution assumes the responsibility for basic library functions and services within another agency or institution, it should be done on a contractual basis that clearly delineates what areas of institutional and agency responsibility and authority are being delegated and the policies and procedures that are to govern the agreement. Such agreements should be regarded as interim or stop-gap measures rather than as desirable long-term solutions.

It might be advantageous and desirable for the institution to make arrangements for *supplementary* services (such as bookmobile service, loan of films and other materials, assistance in special programs, special services for staffs) from neighboring public, school, academic, or special libraries. Library staff in institutions should maintain professional association with other library staffs and professional activities in the area and seek to develop cooperative activities.

Working for the development of state institutional library service is analogous to the way in which a state library agency works for public library development and larger units of service. Essential to a successful program are such activities as: the assessment and interpretation of library needs; the cooperative development of plans and policies through discussion with agency officials; the defining of the supervisory and administrative function and resources of the state agency responsible for institutional service and the plan for personnel, collections, and service within each institution; continuing and consistent advisory and consultative services to the agency including participation in in-service training programs for library staffs, supplying supplementary resources and services, and bringing institution libraries into the total state interlibrary cooperative network. It is the unique job of the state library agency to see that the specialized needs, rather than the general day-to-day interests, of staff and residents are met through state library agency resources and the development of interlibrary cooperative arrangements, and to bring these agencies into other cooperative activities such as centralized technical processing, evaluation of materials, and in-service education. In the long run, institutional libraries will become valuable forces in the rehabilitation and treatment of residents to the extent that they are able to perform their own respective functions and to become an integral part of the larger network of available resources and services.

INDEX